A 3-minute forever book

EAT
YOUR
PEAS®

for Birthdays

By Cheryl Karpen
Gently Spoken Communications

A gift for

from

Being pretty on the inside means
you don't hit your brother
and you
eat all of your peas
⌒ that's what
my grandma taught me.

−Lord Chesterfield

Of all the good people
born on this day
since birthdays were invented
no one, absolutely no one,
can hold a candle to you
and what you mean
to the people in your life.

I am so very glad to be one of them!

So I'm giving you
this little book
to remind you
how important you are to me.

Every day.
All year long.

Read often for maximum smiles!

Close your eyes.
Can you hear me singing?

Happy Birthday to you,
Happy Birthday to you,
Happy Birthday dear
,

Happy Birthday to you!

How can I possibly
contain my
celebration of you
to just one day?

Take your party with you wherever you go.

Party!

(That way you'll always be ready to celebrate what life sends your way.)

# Candles. Candles. Candles.

Count 'em if you want to.
Blow them out if you don't.

You are as young
as you feel.
As grown up as you
want to be.
And it's okay to mix them up.

To cake or not to cake.
That is the question.

(I say two pieces are the absolute minimum.)

May your capacity
for
**joy**
be multiplied by
the number of candles
on your
cake.

Unwrap this day.

Savor it.

May
grace *and* gladness
fill each day
of your life.

Take time to
*daydream.*

You'll never know how
far you might go or what
you'll bring back.

At least once this year,
get up early to
watch the sun come up

and stay up late enough
to watch for

shooting stars

You are an
amazing
person
worthy of
celebration
every day.

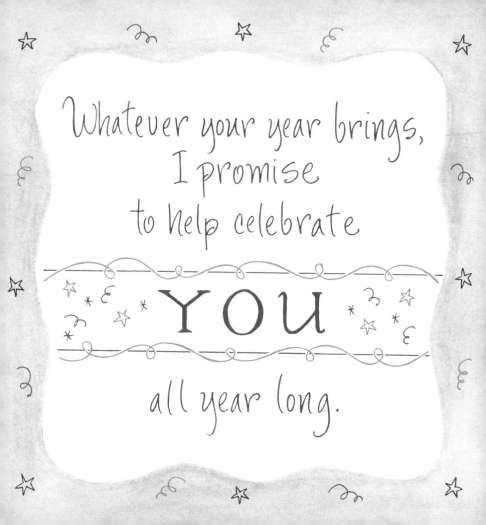

Whatever your year brings,
I promise
to help celebrate

YOU

all year long.

This is your birth-day.

It truly
is
a special day.

Indulge yourself a little.

Or a lot.

No one deserves it more!

Most of all
take good care of yourself...

Remember
to
eat your peas...

and your cake!

## Why Peas?

She was a vibrant, dazzling young woman with a promising future.
Yet, at sixteen, her world felt sad and hopeless.

I was living over 1800 miles away and wanted to let this very special young person in my life know I would be there for her across the miles and through the darkness. I wanted her to know she could call me any time, at any hour, and I would be there for her. And I wanted to give her a piece of my heart she could take with her anywhere—a reminder she was loved.
**Really loved.**

Her name is Maddy and she was the inspiration for my first PEAS book, **Eat Your Peas for Young Adults**. At the very beginning of her book I made a place to write in my phone number so she knew I was serious about being available. And right beside the phone number I put my promise to listen—really listen—whenever that call came.

Soon after the book was published, people began to ask me if I had the same promise and affirmation for adults. I realized it isn't just young people who need to be reminded how truly special they are. **We all do.**

Today Maddy is thriving and giving hope to others in her life.
If someone has given you this book, it means **you are pretty special** to them and they wanted to let you know. Take it to heart.

Believe it, and remind yourself often.

Wishing you peas and plenty of joy,

Cheryl Karpen

P.S. If you are wondering why I named the collection, Eat Your Peas…it's my way of saying, "Stay healthy. I love and cherish you. I want you to live **forever!**"

Sprouting our seventeenth title,
**Eat Your Peas for Birthdays** is truly a celebration
of the power of encouragement and affirmation
to touch hearts and lives.

## Special thanks to:

Artist **Sandy Fougner**,
who creatively and lovingly hand-illustrates each page;
editor **Suzanne Foust**, whose passion for words
makes every PEAS book unique and special;
and to our amazing operations manager,
**Andrea Auel**, for keeping it (and me!) all together.

Each and every day, I count my blessings
because you are part of my life and my dreams.

~CK

If this book has touched your life,
we'd love to hear your story.
Please send it to:
mystory@eatyourpeas.com
or mail it to:
Gently Spoken
PO Box 45
Anoka, MN 55303

## About the author

"Eat Your Peas"

A self-proclaimed dreamer, Cheryl
spends her time imagining and creating
between the historic river town of Anoka, Minnesota
and the seaside village of Islamorada, Florida.

An effervescent speaker, Cheryl brings inspiration,
insight, and humor to corporations,
professional organizations and churches.
Learn more about her at: www.cherylkarpen.com

## About the illustrator

Sandy Fougner artfully weaves
a love for design, illustration and
interiors with being a wife
and mother of three sons.

Other books by Cheryl Karpen

## The Eat Your Peas Collection™

is now available in the following titles:

Daughters　　　　Girlfriends
Sons　　　　　　　Someone Special
Mothers　　　　　Holidays
Fathers　　　　　　New Moms
Sisters　　　　　　Tough Times
Grandkids　　　　Sweethearts
Grandparents　　　Me
Teachers　　　　　Teens

New titles are SPROUTING up all the time!

## Heart and Soul Collection

To Let You Know I Care
Hope for a Hurting Heart
Can We Try Again? Finding a way back to love

To view a complete collection, visit us on-line at **www.eatyourpeas.com**

# Eat Your Peas® for Birthdays

Printed in the USA

For more information or to locate a store near you, contact:
Gently Spoken
PO Box 245
Anoka, MN 55303

Toll-free 1-877-224-7886 or visit us on-line at
www.eatyourpeas.com